HERTFORDSHIRE VOL I

Edited by Dave Thomas

First published in Great Britain in 1999 by
POETRY NOW YOUNG WRITERS
1-2 Wainman Road, Woodston,
Peterborough, PE2 7BU
Telephone (01733) 230748

HB ISBN 0 75430 317 9
SB ISBN 0 75430 318 7

FOREWORD

With over 63,000 entries for this year's Cosmic competition, it has proved to be our most demanding editing year to date.

We were, however, helped immensely by the fantastic standard of entries we received, and, on behalf of the Young Writers team, thank you.

Cosmic Hertfordshire Vol I is a tremendous reflection on the writing abilities of 8 & 9 year old children, and the teachers who have encouraged them must take a great deal of credit.

We hope that you enjoy reading *Cosmic Hertfordshire Vol I* and that you are impressed with the variety of poems and style with which they are written, giving an insight into the minds of young children and what they think about the world today.

CONTENTS

Applecroft School

Kirsty Brettell	1
Emily Buckley	1
Rosalie Watt	2
Thomas Wodcke	2
Gemma Newcombe	3
Ryan Rampton	3
Catherine Bowyer	4
Michelle Johnson	4
Anna Nicholls	5
Rebecca Falla	5
Kikko Kawashima	6
Craig Arnold	6
Gina Rolland	7
Katie Webster	7
Gregg Roantree	8
Jack Elmer	8
Jack Grundy	9
Shannon Bird	9
Louise Newton	10
Rebecca Hayden	10
Anthony Fawcett	11
Rory Page	11

Dundale JMI School

Lily Ingrey	12
Bethany Jones	12
Robyn Kemp	13
Richard McKenna	14
Katherine Armstrong	14
Emma Lampard	15

George Street JMI School

Liam Jahn	16
Michael Houghton	16

Kathryn Ansell 17
Sean Halsey 17
Samuel Chaplin 18
Hannah Thompson 18
Dante Ierubino 19
Roxanne Ghajar 19
Charlotte De Jong 20
Christopher Lawley 21
Kirsty Long 21
Samantha Wells 22
Robert Davies 22
Alice Harding 23
Ben Humphrey 23
Amy Lilley 23
Caylee Burton 24
Dean Stidston 24
Stephanie Payne 25

Great Gaddesden JMI School
Frances Gilbert 25
Joshua Waites 26
Benjamin Stowe 26
Kit Wales 27
Lara MacCrimmon 27
Laura Frewin 28
Rosie Selkirk 28
Luke Brackenbury 29
Sophie Teden 30
Thomas Braggins 30
Laim Ivory 31
John Baker 31
Alice Dickson 32
Natasha Chapman 32
Elizabeth Gilbert 33
Jem Royal 34

Hazelgrove JMI School

Samantha Collier	34
Charlotte Young	35
Carly Shephard	36
Zoe Baker	36
Katie Jupp	37
Chantel Lees	38
Mikala Etches	38
Ben Ebbrell	39
Katie Doran	40
Perry Thornhill	40
Lyndsay Haynes	41
Sam Callan	42
Jack Hughes	42
Laura Davis	43
Charlotte Camm	44

Knutsford JMI School

Natalie Insole	45
Jake Cox	45
Corinne Cox	46
Thomas Freeman	46
Dominic Weerdmeester	47
Hannah Wilkinson	48
Lloyd James	48
Kim Gallichan	49
Faye Rutledge	49
George Inett	50
Kelly Gallagher	50
Blake Smith	51
Megan Blande	51
Colin Ross	52
Stefan Deacon	52
Stephanie Hawkes	53
Danielle Thorpe	53
Gurdeep Seyan	54
Ryan O'Connor	55

Katie Faulkner   55
Matthew Muré   56
Nicola Fowler   56
Amy Watts   57
Faye Smith   57
Perry Byrne   58
Helen Freeman   58
Francesca Lyons   59
Louise Trueman   59
Fay Liberty   60

Lockers Park School

    Max Stivens   60
    Peter Bradnock   61
    Piers Mundy   61
    Jack Rhodes   62
    Robert Stoner   62
    Charlie de Rivaz   63

Manland Primary School

    April Garrihy   63
    Anthony Cole   64
    Georgia Martin   64
    Guy Arnold   65
    Ben Strowman   65
    Sophie Ferrett   66
    Ben Cobb   66
    Kirsty Eddison   67
    Tom McCretton   68

Maple JMI School

    Freddie Clegg   68
    Ben Rosen   69
    Todd Davidson   69
    Jack Irish   70
    Joanna Brown   70
    Joanna Oram   71

Michael Dean	71
Leo Gibbon	72
Freya Gabbutt	72
Ben Goodyear Irish	73
Jonathan Smith-Squire	73
James Clifft	74
Patrick Dulieu-Clark	74
Jonathan Hersom	75
Max Glover	75
Christopher Cooper	76
Jack Elward	76
Lorna Taylor	77
Chloë Barnard	77
Michael Macleod	78
Charlotte Dulieu-Clark	79
Rosie Morgan	80

Margaret Wix JMI School

Jason Hollands	80
Sally Smith	81
Ritchie Aylett	81
Hannah Woods	82
Gemma Watmore	82
Magie Wu	83
Sallie Farrow	83

Meldreth CP School

Karis Wilkins	84

Panshanger School

Gaelah Diab	84
Ross Millson	85
Charlie Cook	85
Rachel Winwood	86
Lewis Bowden	86
Rosie Swanson	87
David Cockram	87

Samantha Nash   88
Stephanie Searle   88
James Day   88
Rebecca Healy   89
James Pethybridge   89
Laura Clark   90
Jenifer Robinson   90

St Adrian's RC JMI School, St Albans

Alicia Kuczmierczyk   91
Lydia Mallinson   92
Sean Dodge   92
Sian Connolly   93
Sophie Anderson   93
Joanna Lewin   94
Claire-Louise Hill   94
Michelle Nash   95
David Gibbons   95
Michael Devine   96
Sarah Torrens   97
Nicola Rudd   98
Jonathan Liddle   98
Krina Patel   99
Robert Tominey   100
Naomi Brice   101
Sam Brzeski   102
Charlotte Shannon-Little   102
Sophie Lovett   103

St Dominic RC JMI School, Harpenden

Eleanor Sheridan   103
Ciaràn Owens   104
Christen Williams   104
Helen Bentley   105
Andrew Kelly   106
Emma Creighton   106
Louise Thompson   107

Adam Davies   108
Matthew Whitworth   109

St John's CE JMI School, Welwyn Garden City
Rebecca Costello   109
Benjamin John Cole   110
Chris Humphreys   110
Geoffrey Pritchard   111

St Margaret Clitherow RC School, Stevenage
Grant Hailey   111
Elizabeth Mulhall   112
Andrew Kennedy   112
Ryan Inglis   113
Sam Harte   113
Bethany McGloin   114

Sacred Heart School
Sarah Hill   114
Jenny Campbell   115
Helen Lawrence   116
Louise Frost   116
Olivia Jane Ferrigan   117
Jianna Miserotti   118
Thomas Gibbons   118
Sara Noone   119
Stuart Jordan   120
Hazel Boland-Shanahan   121
Marisa Rabbini   122

Two Waters School
Niall Galvin   123
Oliver Martin   123
Joshua Taylor   124
Nicholas Mills   124
Sam Nicholls   125
Jason Remmington   125
Lara Peasnell   126

Billy Dove   126
Jody Coffey   127
Lauren Morris   128
Charlotte Wright   128
Jonathan Munday   129

THE POEMS

THE MAN FROM THE MOON

Did you know about the man from the moon?
He eats green moondrops every afternoon!
He invited me up to see the moon,
I said 'Wow wee, I better go soon!'
So when I went on June 12th,
He gave me green moondrops I said 'What else?'
He said 'You can have more moondrops or some cheese,'
I said 'No thanks' and 'Yes please.'
Then he took out a grey can.
I said 'What's that in your hand?'
He said 'It's the moondrops or don't you want them?'
I said 'Yes please in fact I want ten!'
From that day on I've remembered him,
His moondrops, cheese and old grey tin!

Kirsty Brettell (9)
Applecroft School

COSMIC

The rocket has blasted way up high,
Almost touching the magical blue sky.
Past Neptune and Pluto,
Coming up to Jupiter too
The shiny moon is smiling back at you.
The stars twinkled as they floated through space
At the most outstanding pace.
Mars winked at them as they rushed on
But now it's all back in the past.

Emily Buckley (7)
Applecroft School

THE ALIEN GANG

Alert! Alert! It's the alien gang!
Their eyes are coal,
And that moon-white fang,
Look at the aliens,
Help! Oh help!
Save me please!
Don't take me to the galaxies,
Not Neptune not Mars,
Not the planets or the stars,
I hate the alien gang,
I hate the little things,
All they are is blobs of slime,
That try to capture you,
But don't every time,
Can't they just go away today?

Rosalie Watt (9)
Applecroft School

THE PLATE AND SPOON ON THE MOON

The plate and the spoon went up to the moon
And found it was so boring
So they went to Mars and ate jam in jars
Till their tummies were full and started snoring
Then when they woke up they saw an alien
Tall and thin
They rushed to a spaceship and ran right in
When they got home they found an alien bone
And threw it in the bin.

Thomas Wodcke (7)
Applecroft School

SPACE

I went to space one day,
I sat down on Mars,
The moon and stars were shining,
Like cats' eyes in the dark,
All the planets are like footballs,
Up there in the universe,
Where the planets are red and brown,
And are always floating around.

My spacecraft that I ride in,
Is green and black and brown,
I like orbiting around the planets,
The planets Jupiter and Mars,
Space is really excellent,
Up there above the clouds,
I like it, it's really delightful,
And when I go back there,
I will sit down on the moon.

Gemma Newcombe (9)
Applecroft School

COSMIC

The alien from planet Mars
I zoom up to space
I zoom past Jupiter and Mars
I turn back and think
I shall obey the sun and the moon.

Ryan Rampton (8)
Applecroft School

SPACE ROCKET

S illy aliens bite their toes
P lanets in the dark
A stronauts flying in the solar system
C old rocks lying in Mars
E xciting rockets firing with flames

R oller skating aliens racing round the moon
O ctopus astronaut, King of the solar system
C atch the planets running about
K ittens are the best pets space has ever had
E xciting planets swirling round and round
T winkling stars sparkling in the solar system.

Catherine Bowyer (8)
Applecroft School

COSMIC

I'm riding along in my spaceship
For all the world to see.
As I whiz past the moon and stars
It seems as if space never ends.
Look there's the moon but the Earth is bigger
Watch out for Mars!
I wonder what happens on Mars.
Do they have jelly all wobbly in your belly
And bright red jam in jars?
I wonder what happens on Mars.

Michelle Johnson (8)
Applecroft School

COSMIC

On a dark blue night a rocket
blasted off with fright,
Like a magical storm of dust,
Through the sparkling stars above,
So much smoke it left behind,
Flames roared out the back crackling all the way,
The rocket stepped onto the moon one night
and gave some tickets to pay,
It did seem such a long way,
The aliens thought they were amazing,
The astronauts thought the moon was blazing,
They baked cakes in front of their plates and
carried them with snakes,
The green aliens said 'Bye bye,'
The rocket whizzed down to Earth into the deep dark sky,
Then they dropped down on Earth.

Anna Nicholls (7)
Applecroft School

COSMIC

C is for cosmic out there in space.
O is for orbit the Earth goes round the sun.
S is for star way up above.
M is for Mars god of war.
I   is for intergalactic spaceship whizzing round in space.
C is for comet shooting round about.

Rebecca Falla (8)
Applecroft School

COSMIC

The astronaut in space,
Was walking at a slow pace,
When his spaceship whizzed and wheened away.
The alien said,
'You must go to bed,'
So he slept on the moon,
In a crater which looked like a spoon.
But he couldn't wake up,
Even though he cried, *'Hup'*
With a telescope we can still see him lying there,
And that is very, very rare.

Kikko Kawashima (7)
Applecroft School

THE PLANETS

The planets in space don't have any grace,
So they wash their toes as well as their nose,
They hit their arms with their small little palms,
They tell a joke and give him a poke,
They have a race right up in space,
In bed at night they have no fright,
They say a prayer with nothing to wear,
And in the morning they stop snoring,
In the middle of lunch they take a crunch,
They read and weed and sing a song all day long.

Craig Arnold (8)
Applecroft School

COSMIC POEM

10, 9, 8, 7, 6, 5, 4, 3, 2, 1,
Blast off, up up and away,
here goes the zooming rocket,
far far away,
up in the universe through the orbiting planets,
carry on going land on the moon,
carry on going and I'll land on Neptune,
here I was playing my fiddle,
on the colourful planet,
making such a jolly tune,
I felt like going back to the moon,
to eat my food with a silver spoon
on that adventurous day.

Gina Rolland (8)
Applecroft School

SPACECRAFT

S ee an eight-legged animal,
P eace you do not have,
A n alien in sight,
C an you not hurt me,
E ggs to eat, is there?
C ertainly not, there is no food,
R un back to the spacecraft,
A way I say,
F rom space to Earth I go,
T oo ill to do it again.

Katie Webster (8)
Applecroft School

THE SPACESHIP LANDED ON MARS!

The angry dragon began to breathe fire,
Its body shook as it went higher.
The noise was deafening as its roar got louder
As it headed to the sky, its speed got faster.
The spaceship travelled through the stars,
Then took a wrong turning and landed on Mars.
The astronauts stepped onto the Martian ground,
And there in front of them they found,
A surface covered in sherbet saucers, Milky Ways and Mars bars.
The rocket was filled with lots of sweets,
There was hardly room for the astronauts to squeeze in their seats.
Three, two, one, the spaceship lifted off,
And returned to Earth and orbited aloft.
The Martian treats to Earth were hurled,
And children enjoyed sweets that were out of this world!

Gregg Roantree (8)
Applecroft School

COSMIC

When I was in space
I hit my face in a place
And it was cold
And I went to get my pizza
I found it was in my face
I ran out of fuel
And I dashed into mars
With a million chocolate bars
Then I met an alien with fuel
Then I took off again in my rocket.

Jack Elmer (7)
Applecroft School

COSMIC

S hooting stars zooming about in space
P lanets in the solar system
A stronauts zooming up to space in rockets far far away
C omets zooming about in the solar system
E ating cheese on the moon in space

A crobatic aliens swinging about in the solar system
L ittle aliens sitting on Mars eating chocolate bars
I ncredible aliens with two thousand eyes
E arth spinning around very slowly
N eptune zooming around turbo getting hit by rocks.

Jack Grundy (7)
Applecroft School

COSMIC

Shooting stars heading for Mars,
Astronauts on Mars eating chocolate bars,
Aliens on the moon eating with a spoon,
Meteorites on the moon meeting with a spoon,
Have you been to Mars?
I was taking off in a rocket,
Silly aliens bouncing around,
Eye-dazzling planets speeding past,
Around and around the planets go,
Shooting stars shooting around in space.

Shannon Bird (7)
Applecroft School

COSMIC

Major Tom from planet Earth
Going off to the moon in his spaceship
Round and round he spins
Twinkling stars were so small
But not now
Up there look there's Mars
Selling chocolate bars
Oh look there's Pars but
It's a long way from Mars
There are aliens on Pars
Now going back to Earth in the spaceship
'Can I go again?' said Tom.

Louise Newton (7)
Applecroft School

COSMIC

S ome space aliens sipping lemonade
P arty time when you dance on the moon
A t the party lots of food for me
C ream on jelly tickles your belly
E at all the cake
S pacemen hear the noise, hear that!
H ear that Bill?
I wonder what's on Mars
P olar bears in jars!

Rebecca Hayden (8)
Applecroft School

COSMIC

The dark place was like space
It was bouncy
I heard a Concorde
It was cold
My dad was bad
I didn't know what to do
So I took my shoe and threw it up
I found a puppy, it barked at me

Cosmic creatures whiz through space
Aliens have ten green eyes
Astronauts race
Dreadful people in space showing their scary face
Bad monsters silly ghouls
Dark and gloomy it is slippery
Mars was a nice place to have chocolate bars.

Anthony Fawcett (7)
Applecroft School

COSMIC

Planets are small, planets are big
But stars are bright and the moon is lit
Every night when you're in bed
The moon will always shine
No one can stop that from happening
The moon might live forever
But do aliens exist?
Life on Mars can surely not exist
Back on Earth
Were we thinking
Or is it true?

Rory Page (8)
Applecroft School

STARS

Stars light up the night
such a beautiful sight.
You look up and see,
the beautiful night with
beautiful stars so bright.
Morning has come,
the bright stars have
gone behind the sun,
night-time has to come
or stars will be gone.
Hours have gone by
night-time is coming.
The stars are bright
and lighting up the night.
A rocket goes up into the night,
he looks up and sees
the galaxy and planets,
but he can see the stars
most of all.

Lily Ingrey (8)
Dundale JMI School

EARTH

Earth is our home to live in.
Earth was a beautiful place but we came to Earth
and polluted Earth.
We killed Earth's colours.
Earth helps us to live our lives.
After what we did to Earth I thought Earth would not help us.
Without Earth we would not live our own life.

Bethany Jones (8)
Dundale JMI School

GALAXY

I set off one night to the galaxy

G alaxy
A steroids
L aunch
A stronaut
X planet
Y ears   Off I went

Far away from home
I went to the stars
Twinkling things they were
I watched all the planets

M ercury
I gnite
L aunch
K aleidoscope
Y ears
W hite dwarf
A steroids
Y ears   Orbiting the sun

You should have seen them
Well there was one strange planet
That was on its side
That was Uranus
Well that was my short journey round the
Milky Way our galaxy

S aturn
P luto
A steroids
C omet
E arth.

Robyne Kemp (10)
Dundale JMI School

ADVENTURE IN SPACE

When you zoom off into space,
you glare at the sun's face.
Even knowing there's life,
there maybe a star shaped like a knife.
The sun glittering like a crystal,
the ocean squirted with a water pistol.
Since it's so dark,
there are shining sparks.
You never know what comes in the future
it could suit you.
I wonder who created planets?
I wonder who span it?

Richard McKenna (9)
Dundale JMI School

OUT IN SPACE

Out in space
When the stars have a race
And the planets are spinning around
I'm in bed with a dream in my head
Making not a sound.

Down here on Earth
When the sun's in the sky
And the children are messing around
Up in space the planets have a race
And Mercury is the fastest one.

Out in space
Where the stars don't shine
And the Earth is lit by the sun
I'm at school learning nothing at all
Having a lot of fun.

Katherine Armstrong (9)
Dundale JMI School

JOURNEY THROUGH SPACE

Wow I'm in the race of space
Faster and faster the engine goes
Oh no, *ow* it's not that low,
I'm in the journey through space
Down on Earth
The people are whispering will they make it
Or will they not?

We have landed, we have landed
On Jupiter, on Jupiter
Bump bump, check the fuel, *ah ow*
We are very low
Now panic, *ahhhh*
We're falling, we're falling
We now just panic
Now we've stopped panicking
OK we're there.

Emma Lampard (8)
Dundale JMI School

FIREWORK DISPLAY

A whiz bang
A fizz wang
A fun twang
A scary spin
A dad's dream
A mum's scream
A neighbour's nightmare
A good barbecue
A funny turn
A coloured sky
A light night
But most of all
I can't get to sleep.

Liam Jahn (9)
George Street JMI School

AN IMAGINARY DISGRACEFUL CREATURE

A hydra's big head,
A tongue bright red,
A pair of horns, sharp and yellow,
Eyes that hypnotise, they also glow.

A colossal huge belly,
Which fills the room when he watches the telly,
Skinny legs with knobbly knees,
Big strong arms to climb the trees.

I call him Blubber!

Michael Houghton (9)
George Street JMI School

SEASONS

Summer has the painted leaves,
Hanging from the lovely trees.
The grass is fresh, fresh as could be,
So we can walk on it, you and me.

Then comes autumn with the rusty leaves,
Blowing in the cold breeze.

But then comes the freezing weather,
And out comes the sharp, sharp heather,
When the snow will thickly lay,
That's when you play on your sleigh.

Spring is near,
It's nearly here,
When the buds pop out,
Then the flowers begin to sprout.
Then once again it's summer.

Kathryn Ansell (9)
George Street JMI School

STARS

If you had a star and dropped it,
It would smash like a chandelier.
The stars are colder than 2000 ice cubes.
If you touch them
The corners will cut you
Stars are fabulous
If we didn't have them
It would be dreadful.

Sean Halsey (9)
George Street JMI School

THE CEMETERY

In the cemetery it was dark,
And I saw a lark,
Going into the tomb, into the gloom.

And I left no mark.
As I went into the dark,
And I saw a ghost,
Guarding his post.

I also thought I would lie,
Down and die,
As I saw a vampire,
Trying to sit,
In a pit,
Under a tombstone.

Samuel Chaplin (9)
George Street JMI School

WINTER

Freezing cold ice on the roads,
People slipping everywhere losing loads.
The nights seem longer every day,
It's fun, children run to play and shout.
Winter's here and there!
Winter will be over once more!

Hannah Thompson (9)
George Street JMI School

SEA SHORE

One day in a wondrous land,
A crab lay flat on some yellowy sand.
The fish jump high,
The dolphins whoosh,
Through the water and ripples and push.
The sea so calm,
The beach so dry
There's no one there so I could cry.
The seagulls flap overhead,
If you come back it will all be *dead!*

Dante Ierubino (9)
George Street JMI School

AUTUMN

Autumn is coming,
The birds are singing,
The leaves come down,
Scattering around.

The leaves are colours,
Brown, orange, red.
Autumn is cold,
Like an autumn bed!

Roxanne Ghajar (9)
George Street JMI School

ROBIN THROUGH THE YEAR

Robin in the spring,
Happy and merry,
Because winter is over,
He sings a song like wedding bells,
To see his children play.

Robin in the summer,
Happy as can be,
Fly down into the huge green jungle,
That the giants walk on,
With shoes of holes.

Robin in the autumn,
Matches with the leaves,
Dodging them back and forth,
Until the trees are bare,
From top to bottom.

Robin in the winter,
At Christmas time is jolly,
He sings a song like bluebirds in spring,
But after that he gets cold and sad,
And has trouble to fly in the cold wind.

Robin has lived one year through
Spring, summer, autumn, winter.

Charlotte De Jong (9)
George Street JMI School

DOLPHINS IN NEED

D olphins in need
O h they're away in the lead
L ove is sweet
P lease hear my heartbeat
H earing them sigh
I n near time that goes by
N obody cares
S o nobody stares

I n need they may be
N obody can see

N eedless to say
E ternity they stay
E ternity strong
D on't stay away too long.

Christopher Lawley (8)
George Street JMI School

AUTUMN

Autumn winds do strongly blow,
dropping leaves as they go.
Rustling, rustling all around,
autumn leaves lay on the ground.
Hedgerow animals hide away,
to escape the cold, cold day.
Tummies full they're off to sleep
until the sunshine in does creep.

Kirsty Long (9)
George Street JMI School

DADS

Dads, who needs them?
I do!
You do?
Yes I do!
But why?
Because they buy you presents for your birthday
And Christmas too,
They moan when you are naughty,
They hug you when you're good.
You still don't think you need them?
Well, you would!
Girls or boys,
They get you toys.
But that's not really all,
The main thing is they love you,
And that's the best of all!

Samantha Wells (8)
George Street JMI School

WINTER

Winter is a time of fun lots of toys for everyone
lots of boys and girls are playing about
having lots of fun with snowball fights,
They see lots of robins and lots of little creatures
while all the birds fly away at night.

Robert Davies (9)
George Street JMI School

DYING

Dying is a time for rest
Dying can be quite a pest
Dying can be quite a shame
It is certainly not a game
I suppose everyone will have to die
But they don't want you to cry.

Alice Harding (7)
George Street JMI School

FIREWORKS

Fireworks go whoosh *bang!*
Crimson, verdant, azure and cream
Whisk them round to gold and silver
All the colours of your dreams
Whoo *bang! Bang! Bang!*
Fireworks whiz up, up, up and away
Sometimes they go whiz, *bang!* Plop
Scarlet, cerulean, emerald and milk-white.

Ben Humphrey (8)
George Street JMI School

SEE-SAW

See-saw, up and down,
Which way to London town?
One foot up, and the other foot down,
That is the way to London town.

Amy Lilley (7)
George Street JMI School

MY LITTLE TEDDY BEAR

My little teddy bear
has big furry ears
a little pink nose and
eyes full of tears
it's nice to cuddle
it's nice to hold
he keeps me warm
when it is cold
when I'm at school
he's on my bed
it's my favourite toy
and its name is Ted.

Caylee Burton (9)
George Street JMI School

THE CROCODILE

On the banks of the River Nile
Lived a hungry crocodile.
Sitting ready in wait
The hot hot sun
A bird overcome
At the speed of light the
Jaws snap tight
By the banks of the River Nile
Lives a satisfied crocodile.

Dean Stidston (8)
George Street JMI School

THERE'S A GIRL I REALLY DON'T LIKE

She thinks she rules the school.
She thinks she acts so cool.
But she just looks a fool.

As a friend she's not that great.
Saying bad things about her mates.
And she always exaggerates.

Sometimes I wish that she
Would be nicer to me.
I always try to make her see
The way friends ought to be.

Stephanie Payne (8)
George Street JMI School

WHAT IS THE SUN?

The sun is a yellow football
Kicked into space,
It is a yellow boulder
Flying through the sky *ace!*

The sun is a Frisbee circling round and round,
It is a penny farthing
Thrown into the town.

The sun is an orange,
As round as can be
It is a ball of fire,
Ouch it burnt!

Frances Gilbert (8)
Great Gaddesden JMI School

WHAT IS THE SUN?

The sun is a yellow football
Kicked across space
It is a yellow boulder
Flying through the sky

The sun is a Frisbee
As it flies around the Earth
It is a clown's nose as it
Never wants to stop

The sun is like a clock
As it ticks it shines across the Earth
It is a rolling boulder as it
Can never be stopped

The sun is an Olympic yellow ring
Shining down on us
It is an orange plate
That circles the sky.

The sun is central heating
As it warms up the Earth
It is a teacake
Nice and hot and soothing.

Joshua Waites (8)
Great Gaddesden JMI School

THE WIND

The tree is like a fox because it sneaks through trees.
The wind is like a cheetah because it is fast.
The wind is like a wolf because it howls.
The wind is like a horse because it gallops.

Benjamin Stowe (7)
Great Gaddesden JMI School

NOCTURNAL ANIMALS

When darkness falls and children sleep
Out from its hole comes a werewolf
It climbs the hill then howls.

When darkness falls and children sleep
Out from its hiding place comes a bat
First it flies high then shrieks as loud as possible.

When darkness falls and children sleep
Out from its hole comes a mouse
First it finds food then has a feast.

When darkness falls and children sleep
Out from its tree comes an owl
It starts chasing the mice that are having a feast.

Kit Wales (9)
Great Gaddesden JMI School

THE WIND

The wind is like a bird
because it swishes through
the trees and blows the
leaves in all directions.
The wind is like a butterfly
because it gently touches the trees.
The wind is like a cheetah
because it runs through the trees.

Lara MacCrimmon (8)
Great Gaddesden JMI School

WHAT IS THE SUN?

The sun is a yellow football
Kicked across space,
It is a yellow boulder
Flying through the sky.

The sun is a Frisbee
Tossed across the universe,
It is a ball of fire
Thrown into the day.

The sun is a ball
That goes up in the day and
Down at night,
It is a rock
Thrown up from a volcano.

The sun is a submarine
That sails through the sky
It is a bowl of tomato soup
Looking nice to eat.

The sun is a yellow Olympic ring
Burning in the sky,
It is an orange
Bouncing up and down in the universe.

Laura Frewin (9)
Great Gaddesden JMI School

NOCTURNAL ANIMALS' POEM

When darkness falls
and children sleep
out from its house
comes the badger
it climbs through the wood
then *bang*.

When darkness falls
and children sleep
out from its hole
comes the hedgehog
it creeps along the pavement
then goes to bed.

Rosie Selkirk (7)
Great Gaddesden JMI School

ANIMAL POEM

If I was a tiger
I'd leap on the hunters.
If I was a wolf
I'd howl all night.

If I was a cheetah
I'd win every race.
If I was a shark
I'd eat all the fish.

If I was a jellyfish
I'd sting everyone.
If I was a leopard
I'd leap as far as I could.

If I was a fish
I'd swim as fast as I could
If I was a dragonfly
I'd eat all the insects.

If I was a bat
I'd be as black as black.
But as I'm a human
I'll just sit and read.

Luke Brackenbury (9)
Great Gaddesden JMI School

THE WIND

The wind is like a fox
Racing around everywhere.

The wind is like a fish
Sailing over the ocean.

The wind is like a tiger
Sprinting around the forest.

The wind is like a dinosaur
Pushing and crashing everything down.

The wind is like a snail
Slowly moving across the ground.

The wind is like a parrot
Squawking in the wind.

The wind is like a crocodile
Snapping every time you go near.

Sophie Teden (8)
Great Gaddesden JMI School

NOCTURNAL ANIMALS

When darkness falls and children sleep
Out from its hole comes a mouse
It runs around in the field
Then it runs back to its hole

When darkness falls and children sleep
Out from its barn comes the bat
It flaps its wings
Then when morning comes it goes back to the barn.

Thomas Braggins (7)
Great Gaddesden JMI School

THE WIND

The wind is like a wolf
because he howls in the night
running through the grass.

The wind is like a rhino
charging across the land.

The wind is like an elephant
big and strong walking
along as it crashes
through the trees.

The wind is like a lion
roaring with all his might
creeping through the city
ready to catch his prey.

The wind is like a bird
because it glides through the air
gracefully as it blows
the trees gently.

Liam Ivory (9)
Great Gaddesden JMI School

STORM

He is horror when he blows.
He spits when he is in a furious temper.
He hates every one of us.

He throws cold paper in winter.
He coughs and makes scary swirly winds.
He hates every one of us.

John Baker (9)
Great Gaddesden JMI School

In The Thirteenth Hour

In the thirteenth hour
ghosts do a terrorising haunted dance
and the wolf howls a scary song.

In the thirteenth hour
the sea evaporates into a small puddle
and ducks begin to sink.

In the thirteenth hour
volcanoes blow into showers of powdered dust
and animals speak a legend of a king.

In the thirteenth hour
man breathes a glowing fire of excessive anger
and a woman dreams that she soars through the sky.

In the thirteenth hour
the red-hot sun burns out like a huge bonfire
and the sky sank coming down to Earth.

Alice Dickson (9)
Great Gaddesden JMI School

In The Thirteenth Hour

In the thirteenth hour
the moon turns into a melting icicle,
dripping onto the murky ground below.

In the thirteenth hour
the flowers start out with beautiful heads
and slowly die down to a seed,
burrowed in the leafy grass.

In the thirteenth hour
books take off to another land,
reading themselves as they go.

In the thirteenth hour
instead of circling around the planets,
the world makes a starry pattern.

Natasha Chapman (9)
Great Gaddesden JMI School

IN THE THIRTEENTH HOUR

In the thirteenth hour
The sun turns off its rays of light
The moon shines into darkness

In the thirteenth hour
The stars fall from the sky
Your eyes turn black with the clap of thunder

In the thirteenth hour
It rains teardrops of sorrow
Horses grow elegant wings

In the thirteenth hour
The face of a child goes as white as the snowqueen's dress
Books read of tales and wonder

In the thirteenth hour
A rainbow smashes like glass
The northern lights disappear eternity

In the thirteenth hour
The water will be wet no more
The heavens opened and out poured the secrets of time.

Elizabeth Gilbert (9)
Great Gaddesden JMI School

WHAT IS THE SUN?

The sun is a yellow football
kicked into space.
It is a yellow boulder
flying through the sky ace.
The sun is a ball of fire
that has been thrown by an alien.
It is a golden nugget
dropped off a planet.

Jem Royal (8)
Great Gaddesden JMI School

OCEAN

In and out the rock pools
that's where the ocean goes.
Up down flowing around it
makes a very pleasant sound.
As the waves crash to land
splashing up against the sand.
The ocean's rising higher
and it gets much wider
that's how the ocean goes.
Between tides it ebbs and flows.
Seagulls flying overhead
looking out for a piece of bread.

Samantha Collier (10)
Hazelgrove JMI School

I WISH I WISH

Netball netball
Such a good sport
I wish I could
I wish I could
Just win one match.

Football football
Such a boring sport
I wish
I wish our team
Could win one match.

Basketball basketball
I wish I could
I wish I could
I just hope I could play.

Swimming swimming
I just love swimming
I wish I could
I wish I could
Just beat Chantel.

Tennis tennis
I just hate tennis
I wish
I wish
There wasn't such a sport.

Charlotte Young (11)
Hazelgrove JMI School

MY FAMILY DRIVE ME INSANE

My brother loves football,
He drives me insane,
He's always playing football,
He's got football on the brain.

My sister loves swimming,
It drives me insane,
She's always talking about swimming
She's got swimming on the brain.

My dad loves fishing,
He drives me mad,
He's always talking about fishing,
So I say *'Shut up, Dad.'*

My mum loves cooking,
She's always baking cakes,
It takes her an hour,
She doesn't care how long it takes.

I love netball
It drives my family insane
I'm always playing netball
I've got netball on the brain.

Carly Shephard (10)
Hazelgrove JMI School

FOOD

I love food
I adore food
But only when I'm in the mood

I like custard and mustard mixed together
My mother likes butter
My brother likes it too

My uncle likes pickle
My auntie likes onion stew

My nan likes jam
My grandad likes ham
But mixed together we have a slam.

Zoe Baker (10)
Hazelgrove JMI School

A LEAF POEM

I can float,
Not a boat.

I'm a leaf,
Not a reef.

I can't rustle,
I can't bustle.

I'm not a bee,
So leave me.

You can walk,
You can talk.

But don't step on me,
I'm not a bee.

I'm a leaf on a tree,
I'm not a beetle, not a flea.
I wish I could walk,
I wish I could talk.

I wish I could fly,
I wish . . . I could die!

Katie Jupp (10)
Hazelgrove JMI School

ONE DAY I WAS VERY CROSS

One day I was very cross,
Because my mother told me off.
The reason was because of this,
I gave my boyfriend a big kiss.
She wasn't very pleased,
Because she said he had fleas.
Mother said fleas are catching,
They cause scratching when the eggs are hatching.
But as it happens she was wrong,
And I was singing a merry song.
The next night we went out on a date,
We danced, talked and we ate
We came home in a carriage,
And talked about our marriage.
Then I awoke with a scream,
It had all been a terrible dream.

Chantel Lees (11)
Hazelgrove JMI School

SWIMMING

I go swimming every day
the floats are everywhere
people splashing splash, splash
the water goes in the air.

Jumping off high boards
making your ears pop
having swimming races
when the lifeguard is giving the pool a mop.

Mikala Etches (10)
Hazelgrove JMI School

POEMS ARE SO DIFFICULT

Poems are so difficult,
What could I write,
I could write about a football match,
Or write about a fight.

I'd write about a school,
Or write about a cat,
I'd write about my grandma,
Who wears a funny hat.

I'd write about a zoo,
Or write about a dream,
I'd write about my teacher,
Or my favourite rugby team.

I'd write about a river,
Or write about a boat,
I'd write about an aeroplane,
Or my waterproof coat.

I'd write about a car,
Or write about a park,
I'd write about a lake,
Or write about the dark.

I'd write about a holiday,
Or write about a fish,
I'd write about the colours,
Or write about my best food dish.

Poems are so difficult,
I never get them done,
But, hey look I've just finished one.

Ben Ebbrell (10)
Hazelgrove JMI School

DOGS AND CATS

Dogs and cats chasing each other to and fro.
Racing each other.
Oh no there's a mouse.
The dog chases the cat.
The cat chases the mouse.
The mouse has got nowhere to go.
Oh no the mouse has seen some cheese.
I hope she doesn't stop to eat it.
Oh no she did.
Then the cat stopped and ate the mouse.
The dog stopped to eat the cat.
Now the dog has no one to chase.
Oh no the lady has found out and she said
I have to put that dog down.
The owners are going to shout at me.
What shall I do?
I think you should not tell the owner
And do not put your dog down
It will make your children sad and they
Will cry and scream.

Katie Doran (10)
Hazelgrove JMI School

BIRDS

A birdie with a yellow bill
Hopped upon the window-sill,
Cocked his shining eye and said:
'Ain't you shamed, you sleepy-head?'

Perry Thornhill (10)
Hazelgrove JMI School

THE WANDERER

I am a wandering river,
Flowing across the land.
I will take you on my voyage,
The route is simply grand.

First I am the raindrops,
Forming my source,
High up in the mountains,
Is the beginning of my course.

I gush along the hillside,
Right up to the top.
I whoosh down steep valleys,
I never, ever stop.

I gradually slow down,
And have an unhurried pace,
But I don't become that sluggish,
Because it's quite an uneven place.

I come across a waterfall,
Ten metres steep,
As I splash over the top,
I notice I've become less deep.

I meander in the lowlands now,
I flood when it rains,
I'm nearing the end of my travels,
I've been all across the plains.

Here comes the end of my journey,
I know my destiny,
I flow into the ocean,
The big blue sea.

Lyndsay Haynes (11)
Hazelgrove JMI School

SHOPPING

Shopping, shopping is the best
With New Look, Oasis beat all the rest

Shopping, shopping is so cool
I'm going to buy myself a big, big pool

Shopping, shopping is so brill
When I go shopping I get a chill

Shopping, shopping is so good
I'm going to buy myself a coat with a hood

Shopping, shopping is so *wow*
My dad will want a bow

Shops, shops are so cool
People will go shopping too.

Sam Callan (11)
Hazelgrove JMI School

SWEETIES

Sweets are yummy,
Sweets are scrummy,
It's a nice treat,
When you eat a sweet.

I love chocolate,
But not when it's out of date.
I love candy,
It makes me feel dandy.

Liquorice is a dish,
Chocolatey after spaghetti.

Fudge is sticky,
It makes me put on weight.
Mars is a friend, a buddy or a mate.

Jack Hughes (10)
Hazelgrove JMI School

RIVERS AROUND THE WORLD

Up and down waves go,
Up, down and around,
The waves go splash against the rocks
Up, down and around.

Waterfalls are pretty
And they start off small in the city
Up and down the waves go,
Up, down and around.

Sometimes it meanders
While water splashes up
Up and down the waves go,
Up, down and around.

Muddy banks and
Rocky banks and old rivers too,
Up and down the waves go,
Up, down and around.

Soon the river goes
Into the big blue sea.
Up and down the waves go,
Up, down and around.

Laura Davis (10)
Hazelgrove JMI School

SHADOWS

When I am in bed at night,
The shadows on my walls,
Are really very scary,
I wish they weren't there at all.

Oh no, only half an hour,
Until I go to bed,
I hope there isn't a full moon,
That's what I surely dread.

My mum has turned the light off,
Look there is a witch,
I'm sure it's just a teddy bear,
I'll go and turn on the light switch.

I see a dragon breathing fire,
As I steal across the floor,
The fire is probably a comic,
And its head an apple core.

Only about a metre,
Until the light is on,
Come on, don't be afraid,
It won't take that long.

Click, phew it's over,
The witch that's over there,
Well its cloak is just a dressing-gown,
My glitter wig its hair.

The dragon; remember,
My pencil case is his head,
My paintbrushes, its fire,
Okay; I'm going back to bed.

Charlotte Camm (10)
Hazelgrove JMI School

44

SPRING

Walking down the road
I look up at the trees
I see the white and pink blossom
Look in people's gardens and smell the flowers
See and hear the bees
When you go to bed
It is lighter than before
When you wake up
It is light too
When you are going in the car past the trees
You see squirrels
When you wake up
It is Easter then you taste the lovely chocolate
I try to touch the hedgehogs
But no I can't they are too spiky
I love spring.

Natalie Insole (8)
Knutsford JMI School

THE SEASHORE

I see hairy crabs on the rocks,
small sea slugs which look like socks,
starfish on the sand,
children like a band,
jellyfish in rockpools,
lobsters scattering about,
shells like horns.

Jake Cox (6)
Knutsford JMI School

SPRING IS HERE

Daffodils like trumpets,
Introducing spring.
Bees are buzzing showing their bright colours,
Warning everything.
Flowers looking up,
Up at the sun.
This is the sign,
Spring's begun.
The sun is a ball of fire,
Blazing hot and red.
The nights are getting brighter,
And it's warmer in bed.
The smell is sweet,
And filling the air.
Flowers' nectar,
It's lingering everywhere.
Butterflies take their first flight
Tortoiseshells and many more.
The colours and the symmetry,
Watch them fly past your door.
The squirrels shout
And they say,
Come out, *come out,*
Come out and play.

Corinne Cox (9)
Knutsford JMI School

SPRINGTIME

In the spring you see bees
flying around the blossom on trees.

In the spring you smell flowers
they'll smell nice for hours and hours.

In the spring you find creatures,
with all sorts of different features.

In the spring you hear birds,
tweeting some sweet birdy words.
Spring is a wonderful time.

Thomas Freeman (8)
Knutsford JMI School

SPRING

Come on, wake up, smell the flowers
Don't stand out there too long,
Otherwise the April showers will get you.
All the hibernating animals are waking up
All the hedgehogs are
Making a taking
For some food,
It's probably because they're in the mood.
The leaves are falling
The blossom is rising,
So come on out
Because it's springtime,
Hurry up you're missing
All the blossom now,
Hurry before the wind
Blows the blossom away.
The bees are coming to take the pollen
From the flowers.
So come on outside
Otherwise you will miss
Springtime!

Dominic Weerdmeester (9)
Knutsford JMI School

SPRING

Blossom, bluebells, daffodils, snowdrops
winter's coming to an end and spring's starting.
Hedgehogs arise and start looking for food.
The nights get shorter and the days get longer.
Baby animals come out and birds start looking for
somewhere to nest.
The daffodils look like a big sun on a green leaf.
The smell of lovely tulips and the smell of spring.
I see a lovely pond with frogs
hopping about in it and butterflies flutter around
my head while ladybirds crawl up my arms.
I hear birds singing 'It's spring it's spring yeah,'
Squirrels wake up and try to find food.

Hannah Wilkinson (9)
Knutsford JMI School

SPRING

Spring is coming
The nights are getting shorter
Flowers are opening
When you go to smell the flowers
They smell lovely
You can see beautiful blossoms
And I can hear birds singing
And animals having babies
And the taste of Easter eggs.

Lloyd James (9)
Knutsford JMI School

WHAT IS PINK?

What is pink? A pig is pink
with a great big stink.
What is blue? Bluebells are
blue with a smell of dew.
What is green? A lizard is green
with camouflage so not to be seen.
What is red? Robins are red
with a nest as a bed.
What is yellow? Bells are yellow
with a very big bellow.
What is black? Pudding is black
with a burnt bit on the back.
What is white? A swan is white
with a twilight sight.

Kim Gallichan (9)
Knutsford JMI School

SPRING

D is for daffodils
A is for animals
F is for flowers
F is for fun
O is for opening blossoms
D is for daisies
I   is for insects collecting pollen
L is for looking forward to Easter
S is for snowdrops dazzling white.

Faye Rutledge (9)
Knutsford JMI School

SPRING IS BACK

Winter's gone, spring is here.
The sun's woken up and the blossom's on the trees
like pretty diamonds shining.
The daffodils are the sun on a stick.
You can hear the birds singing their tune
that spring has begun.
You can smell the flowers
like they want you to smell them.
There are baby bells on the flowers
that ring to call the bees.
The wind blows away the diamonds on the trees.
The sun is getting ready for summer.
The snowdrops are bits of snow asking for more winter.
The birds sing telling everyone that summer's here.

Georgia Inett (9)
Knutsford JMI School

WINTER

Winter winter it really is
Winter when the snow comes
Falling down from the clouds
Above the snow
Glitters and sparkles
Like a piece of gold
I am so proud to be
Lying in my bed
On this cold winter's night.

Kelly Gallagher (8)
Knutsford JMI School

SPRINGTIME

Hear the baby birds tweet tweet
and smell the blossom on the trees.
The hibernating hedgehogs and
sleeping squirrels wake up at this time of year.
I see tulips, daffodils and crocuses.
I feel the wind blowing against my face.
When we get the sunshine
the sun is nice and hot.
When we get the rain
everything gets soaked.
The weather of spring is unpredictable.
The wind is like a person
blowing on my face.
The sun is like a happy man
beaming down at me.
And the rain is like a
sad lady crying on the world.

Blake Smith (8)
Knutsford JMI School

BUBBLE

Bubble is a golden hamster as golden as the sun
his eyes like big black jewels
his claws like little pincers
his toenails as small as crumbs
his tail like a blunt spike
his whiskers like wire
his ears like baby leaves.

Megan Blande (9)
Knutsford JMI School

SPRING

Hedgehog, mind those thorns on him!
Easter is coming,
Chocolate taste in my mouth,
The smell of flowers and blossom,
Wind nearly blowing me over.
No need to have two blankets,
Far too warm!

Golden daffodils with emerald stems,
The baby animals born,
Sun between showers of rain,
The weather not hot not cold,
Just right.

No more snow
No more frost,
No more frostbite,
No more freezing to death,
I can see bees chasing me,
As I pick flowers too.

Colin Ross (8)
Knutsford JMI School

THE TIGER

The tiger stands in a dark barky wood,
With orange fur to camouflage him,
He silently eyes his prey, tail twitching,
His kingdom surrounds him,
Unseen he gets prepared in his dark world,
Then he pounces on his prey.

Stefan Deacon (9)
Knutsford JMI School

SPRING

Blossom on the trees
Like little berries
Daffodils like little snowflakes
Popping out of the ground
With little trumpet horns on the front
Spring is nearly here
Hedgehogs, squirrels and badgers
Coming out from sleep
Bees buzzing round my head
I think spring is nearly here
Crocuses purple pink and blue
Flowers like a tiger with a bit of hair
I feel wonderful about spring
As I smell the glamorous flowers
Spring is now here.

Stephanie Hawkes (8)
Knutsford JMI School

SPRING

I can hear something
Shhh I can hear squirrels going
up and up and up
So I walk on
I can smell the lovely flowers
I can taste it in my mouth
I touch it in my hands
and it is very smooth
I feel it is very cool in the weather
and it is very hot weather too.

Danielle Thorpe (9)
Knutsford JMI School

SPRING

We're walking through a wall
separating winter and spring.

Trees begin to blossom.
Animals awake.
Squirrels awake, daffodils, snowdrops, tulips, crocuses
appear from nowhere.

We're walking through a wall separating
winter and spring.

I smell flowers,
I sense trees growing, as well as days getting longer
Nights getting shorter.

We're walking through a wall separating
winter and spring.

It's getting warmer like a toaster
takes a while to toast its bread.

We're walking through a wall
separating winter and spring.

People looking forward to Easter.
It leads to summer.

We're walking through a wall separating
winter and spring.

Gurdeep Seyan (9)
Knutsford JMI School

SPRING

Winter is over and it's nearly summer, but
what's in between?
It's spring!

The daffodils come out with yellow, green and orange
onto this flower.
It's spring!

The blossom in the trees, pink and white also faint-red.
The grass long and waiting to be cut after a long winter.
It's spring!

The new birds and bees come out squawking in the early hours
and collecting pollen.
It's spring!

Ryan O'Connor (9)
Knutsford JMI School

QUEEN VICTORIA

V ery beautiful
I n her palace she welcomes you
C onsiderate
T he most generous lady in the world, but strict
O ptimistic
R eigned for 63 years
I ntelligent
A very clever woman.

Katie Faulkner (9)
Knutsford JMI School

NICOLA

Nicola is yellow because she's always cheerful,
Nicola is a radio and is always excited,
If Nicola was a flower she would be a rose,
Because she is always bright,
Nicola is a cheetah hunting for her prey,
Nicola's favourite time is 8.55am as she's always on time,
Nicola is a hawk flying in the air, gliding side to side,
Nicola is a footstool because she's sometimes lazy,
Nicola is a sun, hot and bright,
Nicola is Spain because it's a nice hot country.

Matthew Muré (9)
Knutsford JMI School

HARBIND

If Harbind was a colour he would be grey.
If Harbind was a piece of furniture he would be an old coffee table
with dust on it.
If Harbind was a time of day he would be 9 o'clock in the morning.
If Harbind was a flower he would be a holly tree.
If Harbind was a kind of weather he would be thunder and lightning
because he likes noises.
If Harbind was a criminal he would be a bat.
If Harbind was a bird he would be a pigeon in the High Street.
If Harbind was my pet he would be a budgie because he talks too much
If Harbind was a cartoon character he would be Tweety Pie.

Nicola Fowler (9)
Knutsford JMI School

STEFAN

Stefan is red, he's angry.
He would be a lampshade for light.
He would be 3.15pm, he likes going home.
He would be a tiger lily, he races round like tigers.
He would be hailstones, he always runs around.
He would be a tiger, he roams round.
He would be a woodpecker, he will never sit still.
He's a hot curry with peppery sauce.
He's boiling Kenya.
He's Tasmania, he's always talking about it.

Amy Watts (10)
Knutsford JMI School

ZOKON

Boing, boing, boing jelly floor bouncing up and down.
Waterfalls going up, up, up.
Half-eaten metal spoons.
A black, dark rainbow,
It's colourful at noon but dark at night.
Unstable floor.
Smelly grass be careful, get a mask.
The sun is dark shining on the rocks.
The houses are melting by the cold black sun.

I think I'm dreaming!

Faye Smith (9)
Knutsford JMI School

ZOBA

Coloured stars in the light.
The colours of the moon in the night.
Glittering waterfalls rising up the hill.
In the valley of big blue bill.
The melting colours of the rainbow.
In the warm snow.
Orange silky surface and the blue rocks.
And the colours of the farmers' flocks.
Green and orange glazes and the stained glass.
And the colours of the glittering grass.
Two massive big blue suns, one cold, one hot.
With a star with a great big spot.
Now the light has gone.
From when it had shone and shone.
Now the planets flow and flow.
It's now time for me to go.

Perry Byrne (9)
Knutsford JMI School

THE TIGER

His golden, auburn coat of fur,
With specks of coal and snow,
Gleaming as his eyes dart around like flashes of lightning.

He hides away in a cloud of colour,
Grasses waving like hands,
Pounces with great ease to catch his unsuspecting prey.

Helen Freeman (9)
Knutsford JMI School

THE LITTLE CLOUD'S DREAM

As the little cloud lies asleep safe and sound,
His dream is just so wicked but very, very quiet.
In his dream he's fighting but his friend the wind is dead.
The little cloud lies alone racing all around.
Then suddenly the sun comes and the little cloud dies.
As the sun takes over ruling all the world.
He wakes up with a scream and the sun is really there.
The little cloud starts to run but the sun is just too quick
and the cloud's life is done.
The sun takes over and his business starts to run.

Francesca Lyons (9)
Knutsford JMI School

SUN

As hot as a bonfire
As yellow as the sand
As bright as a torch in the dark
Bright, burning, scorching,
Makes people rush to get their swimming pools out,
Beaming, round, a suntan maker, dangerous, a big scorcher, beautiful,
Makes people happy, lights up the sky,
Snow-melter, as round as a yellow sphere, dries up water.

Louise Trueman (9)
Knutsford JMI School

THE TIGER

As he stands, alert and frozen,
Watching, waiting for a chance to kill,
His only movement, his slow, steady breathing.

The grass around him sways in the wind,
The trees, watching, waving, waiting,
And then he jumps, flying through the air like a bird.

Fay Liberty (9)
Knutsford JMI School

A FRIEND IS . . .

F aithful friends give a stern warning not to wake up too early in
   the morning.
R esponsible friends may be sad but at least they don't make you bad.
I   maginative friends always day-dream that they are angels and
    they gleam.
E xtraordinary friends drive me round the bend.
N aughty friends never blend with me.
D rippy friends don't follow trends.
S mall friends sometimes hope to be tall.

Max Stivens (8)
Lockers Park School

A FRIEND

A friend came over I tried him out,
he looked rather like a Brussel sprout.
I said to myself is this the one,
no way, he's lethal, he's got a gun.

A friend came over I looked at him,
he looked rather like an ugly bin.
I shuddered down to my toes,
then he punched me in the nose.

I went over to a friend's house,
and he was as small as a mouse.
He said to me will you be my friend,
if I don't drive you round the bend?

Peter Bradnock (9)
Lockers Park School

FRIENDS ARE . . .

I have friends who are kind and caring.
I have friends who are funny and have money.
I have a friend who I trust and is called Gus.
I have a friend who is small and plays pool.
I have friends who are crazy and lazy.
I have friends who are smart and come first on the chart.
I have a friend who is sporty and naughty.
I have a friend who is daring and sharing.

Piers Mundy (9)
Lockers Park School

A Friend Would Never Be . . .

A friend would never be a friend,
If they were not fair,
A friend can never be a friend,
If they do not care!

A friend is never ever a friend,
If he laughs when you fall,
A friend cannot be a friend,
If he kicks you down your hall!

A friend just isn't a friend,
If he tries to kill your rat,
A friend is not a friend,
If he feeds it to the cat!

Jack Rhodes (9)
Lockers Park School

A Friend Is . . .

F riend is kind, caring and sharing.
R acing and playing, having fun with you.
I ndoors, outdoors, laughing with you all day long, having fun
   with you.
E ating, drinking, teasing, sneezing doing the stupidest things with you.
N aughty, naughty, crazy, funny on the playground we go.
D o it again he says, so off we go and do it again.

Robert Stoner (9)
Lockers Park School

A FRIEND

I have a very loyal friend,
sometimes he drives me round the bend.
He's crazy, honest, modest and fair.
He's very nice and likes to share.

My friend always sticks up for me,
and has a nice personality.
My friend never boasts you see
and never ever shouts at me.

My friend is very sporty
and is quite naughty.
He is very funny.
He is quite like me.

My friend is quite trustworthy
and would never fight with me.
My friend has sugar in his tea
and will never break-up with me.

Charlie de Rivaz (9)
Lockers Park School

VALENTINE'S DAY

It is fun on Valentine's day when you open your cards
and if you get a present, you are very lucky.
Because not many people get a present on Valentine's day.
I like having chocolates and big cuddly bears.

April Garrihy (9)
Manland Primary School

DOGS

Dogs so cute, cuddly and playful what more could you ask for.
They help the army, the blind and the deaf what more could you ask for.
They lay around all day until you let them out then they pick up the ball
and drop it at your feet.
You pick it up, it's all slimy, you throw it as fast as you can.
They run after it, their feet pounding on the ground as they swiftly run
towards the ball with their lips wobbling like a bowl of jelly.
They finally get to it, they pick it up and run back, a bit floppy because
they're tired.
Instead of running to you they run straight past you into the house.
Then they just lay around the house all day until it's time for
their walk.
When it's time for their walk, they're out of that door before you
can say 'Bob's your uncle!'
They walk up the road so nicely until they see another dog or
person.
Then they nearly pull your arm out of its socket and they jump so high,
they look like they're a kangaroo.
Then you take them home.

Anthony Cole
Manland Primary School

NEVER

Never in the world will there be someone like me.
Never will there be someone exactly the same.
Never will I paint like Picasso or write like Roald Dahl.
Never will I catch a shark or go swimming in the Indian Sea.
Never will I climb Mount Everest or go travelling in faraway lands.
Never will I meet a mermaid or be on TV.
All these things I'll never do because I'm just me.

Georgia Martin (9)
Manland Primary School

SNOW

As I get out of bed and look outside I see nothing but snow.
The world is still, quiet and white.
With my hat and gloves, outside I go.

When I step into whiteness the chill hits me,
My nose and ears turn red.
The snow crunched beneath my feet,
As over the garden I sped.

I feel alone in the silence as I look around,
Not a face, no movement, no sound,
There's nothing to be found in the nothingness of white.

Guy Arnold (9)
Manland Primary School

THE FIRE AND THE CAT

The cat laying by the fire,
Snuggling up.
The fire burning,
Flames pop up.
The smoke goes up the chimney.
The cat's going to sleep now.
The fire is getting bigger.
The cat is warm.
He moves away from the fire
and lays down on the furniture.
Now the cat is cooling down,
So is the fire.

Ben Strowman (9)
Manland Primary School

I'M GOING TO THE ZOO

I'm going to the zoo,
How about you?
Elephants, tigers and monkeys too!
Monkeys eat bananas,
Tigers eat meat,
Elephants eat peanuts,
Just like you!

You're bananas so you'll get on with the monkeys
You're made of meat,
Which tigers like to eat,
Elephants eat peanuts,
Which you like to eat.

They'll be seals doing tricks,
Which I'm sure we can fix,
They'll be drinks,
Made of Weetabix.

I'm going to the zoo,
How about you?
They'll be elephants, tigers and monkeys too!

Sophie Ferrett (9)
Manland Primary School

THUNDERSTORM

There's thunder in the air tonight,
A distant growling, and the light,
Gets brighter with each sudden flash,
Much louder grows the thunder crash.

The storm is almost overhead,
It lightens up Rebecca's bed,
And water gushes down the street,
She hears it, crouched beneath her sheet.

Louder, louder now and peals of thunder,
Swift on lightning's heels,
As if they've to chase away,
The calm of night and bring back day.

Now all is peace, save drips of rain,
And far away a growl again,
Rebecca sighs with great relief,
Such stillness seems beyond belief.

Ben Cobb (9)
Manland Primary School

WINTER WONDERLAND

Winter wonderland, snow covering the trees,
Pine cones covering the ground.
Wind gushing everywhere my ears are going to drop off soon.
Snow softly and daintily landing on my head.
The sun is faintly shining behind some snow-made clouds.
A winter wonderland, holly bushes everywhere.
Let's count up the Christmas trees in houses.
So far I've counted ten, all covered in decorations and balls.
Fires lit with cats sitting in front.
The chimneys are blowing out smoke.
I'm enjoying the snow daintily landing on my head.
I hope I won't freeze too much.
I'm wrapped up nice and warm, a scarf, a pair of gloves, some
earmuffs and a nice woolly hat.
I enjoy the winter but hope spring will soon come.

Kirsty Eddison (9)
Manland Primary School

WHY ARE PARENTS ALWAYS MAD?

In house 31 a movement occurred,
Throughout the night nothing had stirred.
The alarm clock buzzed on half-past seven,
While down at church all were praying to heaven.
Mum got up and pulled our toes,
'Right you slobs, here's your clothes.'
I got up, still half-sleeping,
The thought of work sent Mother weeping.
Dad was cross and very stressed,
Because my brother wouldn't get dressed.
I arrived downstairs all tired and grotty,
And then found out that I'd gone potty.
Half-past eight, nearly school,
I was dressed for the swimming pool!
Mum was yelling, so was Dad,
That's why parents are always mad!

Tom McCretton (9)
Manland Primary School

HOT AND COLD

As hot as a volcano and the lava inside
As cold as snow that drifts down from the sky.
As hot as desert sand, yellow and brown
As cold as ice that people skate on.
As hot as Jupiter that spins round and round.

Freddie Clegg (7)
Maple JMI School

BLACK AND WHITE

As black as coal, you use for a fire.
As white as a seagull, gliding in the sky.

As black as space, with all the planets.
As white as paper, before you write.

As black as a shadow, making you nervous.
As white as snow, drifting around.

As black as soot, rushing down the chimney.
As white as a white board, clean and spotless.

Ben Rosen (7)
Maple JMI School

HOT AND COLD

As hot as lava, racing down the volcano,
As cold as snow, crunching under your feet,
As hot as coal, blazing on the hearth,
As cold as minus 1,000 degrees, freezing you immediately!
As hot as the sun, lighting up the Milky Way,
As cold as Pluto, way out in space!
As hot as the Sahara, with mounds of sand.
As cold as the South Pole with loads of penguins!

Todd Davidson (7)
Maple JMI School

HOT AND COLD

As hot as a stove, sizzling in the kitchen
As cold as an iceberg, floating in the sea.

As hot as a fire, burning in the fireplace
As cold as snow, freezing on the ground.

As hot as the sun, shining down on us
As cold as Russia, a big shivering country.

As hot as a volcano, stretching to the sky
As cold as Pluto, where it's *really* cold!

Jack Irish (7)
Maple JMI School

HOT AND COLD

As cold as an iceberg resting in the sea.
As hot as a volcano exploding.

As cold as an icicle on the roof.
As hot as the desert, it never rains.

As cold as ice-cream in the freezer.
As hot as the sun's rays shining down to Earth.

As cold as ice, slippery on the path.
As hot as a microwave baking pizza.

Joanna Brown (8)
Maple JMI School

THE GLOW OF A CANDLE

Candles, candles,
Glowing bright.
Trickling wax,
From such a height.
Light it quickly,
See the flames.
Different colours,
In different lanes.
Black smoke,
Away from fire.
Burning, burning,
Higher and higher.
Don't forget,
The flowing light.
Always glowing,
Bright, bright, bright!

Joanna Oram (9)
Maple JMI School

ROMANS

R is for roads, Romans built straight ones.
O is for oil, because they didn't have soap.
M is for mosaic, made from small stones.
A is for aqueducts, carrying water.
N is for numerals, numbers in Latin.
S is for soldiers, who won the battles!

Michael Dean (8)
Maple JMI School

THE SEA

Listen to the sea,
Crashing wildly against the rocks.
Look at the sea,
Lovely bluish, greenish colour.
Touch the sea,
Sliding through your hands.
Taste the sea,
Salted.
Feel it tickling you tongue.
Smell the sea,
Smells of crabs' claws and fish.

Leo Gibbon (7)
Maple JMI School

THE SEA

Listen to the sea,
Mashing the rocks away.
Look at the sea,
Rolling to get to land.
Touch the sea,
Seaweed wrapping round your finger.
Taste the sea,
Your mouth swelling with sea water.
Smell the sea,
Full of salt.

Freya Gabbutt (7)
Maple JMI School

HOT AND COLD

As hot as a fire burning red.
As cold as ice freezing cold.

As hot as Mars, very near the sun.
As cold as Pluto, a very chilly planet.

As hot as the sun flashing yellow,
As cold as space all dark and raw.

As hot as a volcano blazing red,
As cold as the snow drifting down.

Ben Goodyear Irish (8)
Maple JMI School

HOT AND COLD

As hot as a volcano, lava pouring out,
As cold as a fridge, freezing me to death.

As hot as a sizzling sausage, roasting in a pan,
As cold as ice-cream, melting in your hand.

As hot as a desert, the lizards live there,
As cold as snow, when you make a snowman.

As hot as Lanzarote, you will need a cold drink!
As cold as an iceberg, floating in the sea.

Jonathan Smith-Squire (8)
Maple JMI School

THE SEA

Listen to the sea,
Crashing against the rocks.
Look at the sea,
Blue and green,
Smashing against the breakwaters.
Touch the sea,
Cold as seaweed brushing against you.
Taste the sea,
Salty, scaring your tongue like nothing on Earth.
Smell the sea,
Of seaweed and dead fish.

James Clifft (8)
Maple JMI School

HOT AND COLD

As hot as lava exploding out of a volcano.
As cold as an iceberg floating in the Antarctic.
As hot as the sun lighting the Earth.
As cold as Pluto the coldest thing in the universe.
As hot as Jupiter a scorching place.
As cold as the freezer with lots of ice.
As hot as the oven with blazing heat.
As cold as an ice-cube melting in our drink.

Patrick Dulieu-Clark (8)
Maple JMI School

MAGIC BOX IN AUTUMN

I will put into my box,
The brown leaves of autumn
The colour patchwork of leaves
And the white, white smell.

I will put in my box,
A magic rainbow,
The sound of the wind,
Whistling and howling.
The gorgeous perfume of fruit.

I will put into my box,
The smoke from the first bonfire,
The smell of the sap from a tree.

Jonathan Hersom (9)
Maple JMI School

FLAME

Flickering, dancing in the light.
Glowing, shining. Wax trickling
down the candle. Down, down. It
seems to represent lightning the
sun and lava. It seems to look at you.
Mystical, magical. It represents city
lights, street lamps, advertisements
and TV. It is the symbol of stars, the
moon and explosions. It is a badge of
natural lights and artificial light and
many others beside. It says to me
'Look at me!' This candle never ends.

Max Glover (9)
Maple JMI School

Autumn Box

I will put into my box,
The crispy golden wheat fields.
The white cold misty morning.
The brown and red leaves drifting in the trees.

I will put in my box,
The sweet smell of the fresh ripe fruit.
The white smell of smoke.
The leafy brown crispy smell.

I will put into my box,
The whining trees in the howling wood.
The brushing, shaking branches.
The clicking nuts hitting together.
The crackling fire.

Christopher Cooper (9)
Maple JMI School

Van Gogh Acrostic Poem

V ery good at painting.
A very good artist.
N ever happy.

G reat paintings.
O n his pictures he shaded the colours.
G reat sunflowers, they're my best picture.
H e cut his ear off. He gave it to a lady.

Jack Elward (8)
Maple JMI School

ARACHNE POEM

Small weak and helpless.
Shivering in a high lonely corner.
Cursing herself.
Spinning her silvery-dewed web in the golden sun.
Ripped away every day
By the cleaners, cleaning away.
Every day swept away by the duster shaped like a bun.
Now every spider is called an Arachne.
And now you know why.
So don't boast because you're under God's eyes.
So remember this poem unless you want to be a spider like

Arachne.

Lorna Taylor (7)
Maple JMI School

NASTY LUNCHES

When I put into my mouth my nasty, smelly school lunch,
I hear myself go crunch, crunch, crunch.
I grind my back teeth as I eat.
Then for the big slide,
Squeeze as I ride, ride.
Now for a slosh and a slash with my feet,
But some of us don't care to complete.
Jonah and the whale. *Oh no! Oh no!*
Twisting gracefully round and round,
I feel my heart start to pound and pound.

Chloë Barnard (9)
Maple JMI School

THE STORY OF OSIRIS (PART ONE)

Osiris, kind and fair
Queen Isis, beauty with long black hair
One of these royal, oh Isis loving loyal

Then Seth
Jealous, beastly brother
His evilness beats any other

He offered a chest, made by the best
Whoever could fit it would keep their faces lit
One by one they tried and Osiris sighed
His turn had come, the other people's faces were glum
He fitted the chest, Seth slammed the lid
Osiris shouted like a kid
Seth put it in the Nile that stretches for many a mile

Loving Isis found the chest but Seth did not want to rest
He cut up the remaining pieces of the body and hid them
Isis looked everywhere and found them
She called on god Anubis to give him life
So she would not be a lonely wife

He could not come back to Earth to rule
So he was sent to be a god in the sky
Isis was so sad she began to cry.

Michael Macleod (9)
Maple JMI School

THE AUTUMNAL MAGIC BOX

I will put into my box:
The last brown leaf of an autumn tree.
The brilliant pink and yellow of an autumn sunset.
The magical silver frost on an early autumn morning.
The softest orange of early autumn leaves.

I will put into my box:
The sweet, sharp smell of bursting-open plums.
The smoky smell of a gardener sweeping up dead leaves.
The fresh smell of ripe blackberries.
The sharp smell of juicy strawberries.

I will put into my box:
The sprinkling of a hose on dry autumn soil.
The whispering of the rustling leaves on the playground tree bark.
The whispering and howling of the cold autumn wind, floating
between the trees.
The crackling and sparkling of an early bonfire,

I will put into my box:
The magic of autumn.

Charlotte Dulieu-Clark (9)
Maple JMI School

IN THE PLAYGROUND

I wander around the playground,
With nothing at all to do,
And sit down on the bench,
No one to talk to . . .

Everyone's huddling in corners,
Talking amongst themselves,
Looking and staring at me,
Voices pound my head, like bells.

A teacher blows the whistle,
Everyone pushes and pulls,
Bickering in the cloakroom,
Full with whispers and calls.

More nightmares next break.
Will it always be like this?

Rosie Morgan (11)
Maple JMI School

SCHOOL DINNERS

School dinners are very disgusting.
They look like they come from a dustbin.
I think cheese flan should be banned.
Because it made me sick this morning.
The chips taste like sticks.
The fishcake well, don't eat that
Or you'll soon be in your coffin!

Jason Hollands (9)
Margaret Wix JMI School

MY SLOPPY LITTLE SISTER

My sloppy little sister,
Her name is called Wriggle.
She drinks so much,
She makes herself dizzy.
My sloppy little sister,
Has a very messy bib.
She makes it all milky,
When she is sick.
My sloppy little sister,
She has a very bad temper.
She makes her self go red,
And falls off the chair.

Sally Smith (9)
Margaret Wix JMI School

SCHOOL DINNERS

I think school dinners are rotten
they taste like a bit of cotton.

There are needles in the chicken
and lumps in the mash.

The sausages have green bits
and the pork pies have a chilli taste.

Ritchie Aylett (9)
Margaret Wix JMI School

I Hate ...

I hate school.
I hate work.
I hate teachers that give me homework.

I hate people when they are horrible.
I hate teachers when they're smoking.
Because they're choking.

I hate to go outside when it is cold.
The teachers are all warm inside
They just sit, drink, talk and smoke.
I hate, I hate, I hate.

I hate detentions because they're boring.
I have had one detention so I know what you're feeling.

> *I hate, I hate,*
> *I hate ...*

Hannah Woods (9)
Margaret Wix JMI School

Witch's Pot

In my pot we must put a horrible juicy mouth.
Some are alive, some are dead.
Some are old, some are young.
The stew is green and bubbly.

Be careful when you go near, it is very smelly.
People drink it then they die.
They come alive, alive again.
Alive again with their spirits.

Gemma Watmore (9)
Margaret Wix JMI School

I LOVE , , ,

I love my family.
I love having pets.
I love eating so much.
I love, I love, I love so much,
I love going to school.
I love reading and writing.
I love making friends.
I love, I love, I love so much.
I love helping my mum and dad.
I love doing work.
I love everything on Earth.
I love, I love, I love so much.

Maggie Wu (9)
Margaret Wix JMI School

MY LOVING MOTHER

My loving mother,
Running round the town.
In shops and out shops,
Crawling round the town.
Cooking and looking,
Where she's going to be.
That's my moving mother,
Where is she?
Is she in the market?
Is she in the store?
Why is she always
Running round for me?

Sallie Farrow (9)
Margaret Wix JMI School

Weather Time

Have you felt the wind?
  The spine-chilling wind
    Whirling and spinning around you
      Whistling around on the window-panes
      Have you felt the wind?

Have you seen the lightning?
  Flashing from the sky
    Ablazing the sky with light
      One second it's there, the next it's gone
      Have you seen the lightning?

Have you heard the thunder?
  One clap of thunder, two claps of thunder and more
    It's like an earthquake in the sky
      Never knowing when it's coming.
      Have you heard the thunder?

        Bang!

          See what I mean!

Karis Wilkins (9)
Meldreth CP School

This Planet

This planet is feeling sad and blue,
This planet has got the flu,
This planet is coughing and sneezing,
This planet is absolutely freezing,
This planet gets a letter,
Then it makes him better.

Gaelah Diab (9)
Panshanger School

I WAS ONCE IN BED

I had a rocket
A snazzy US NASA rocket
With all the gadgets you could think of.
With US government atomic missile bombs.
And before I knew it
10, 9, 8, 7, 6, 5, 4, 3, 2, 1 blast-off!
30 g's, 40 g's, 60 g's, 80 g's
And before I knew it
I was in space for the first time.

Well no one my age has been in space before
I saw some aliens and killed them with my laser gun,
NASA gave me a mission
As no other spaceman has done before.
Blew up Jupiter and *kaboom!* No more
Jupiter warships all my missiles are up
Boooooooooom! Oh good it's just a dream!

Ross Millson (8)
Panshanger School

ALIEN FROM MARS

There was an alien from Mars
Who didn't like chocolate bars
He'd tried one before
And crashed to the floor
And said 'I'd rather eat cars.'

Charlie Cook (8)
Panshanger School

THIS ICY PLANET

This cold planet,
It's all lonely,
It's like a wandering pony,
This planet,
It's all icy,
An astronaut fell off it once,
And lost his bounce,
And broke his back,
This planet,
Once lived next to Earth,
But now it's next to Pluto,
It always moves every day,
To a different planet,
All the way,
And learns a new way every day.

Rachel Winwood (9)
Panshanger School

A LITTLE GREEN MAN

A little green man from outer space
Who tripped up and fell flat on his face
He got up and fell over
And landed in Dover
And packed his clothes and his case.

Lewis Bowden (9)
Panshanger School

THE PLANETS ARE GOING CRAZY

It's crazy in this house,
Saturn's got his ring and wants to get married,
Venus wants to be our vicar,
Mars is shouting, getting everyone's attention,
Pluto is arguing like normal with his brothers.
Neptune, Saturn and Jupiter,
Saturn's in two arguments at once,
Now Jupiter's shouting as well,
Mercury wants to get back nearest to the sun,
Hooray! That worked, shouting *stop!* Until my head burst,
I've tried before but now my head exploded,
I got everything right,
And I did like Saturn's ring so he gave me a piece.

Rosie Swanson (8)
Panshanger School

THIS ROCKET

This rocket was in my dream
It was really scary
But I carried on going up.
So I went up and up and up
But then the ignition fell out
And I couldn't find it.
I'm crashing into a planet
Aaaahhhh! Oh no I crashed into Mars!
My spaceship is going to blow.

>   *Bang!*

David Cockram (8)
Panshanger School

THERE WAS A MAN FROM MARS

There was a man from Mars
He bought a bunch of bars
He fell down on his face
And left his case
And came back with broken bars.

Samantha Nash (9)
Panshanger School

THE COLOURFUL MAN

There was a colourful man
Who sat on the moon eating cheese all day.
He got too big and fell off the moon
And sat on a star.
Then *pop!*
He wasn't big any more!

Stephanie Searle (9)
Panshanger School

THESE TWO BOYS

There were once two boys from Mars.
Who had loads of Galaxy bars.
They burped really loud.
And weren't very proud.
And still they would not stop eating Galaxy bars.

James Day (9)
Panshanger School

THIS ALIEN

This alien has gloomy eyes.
This alien has green skins.
This alien has spots on his skin.
This alien has a red mouth.
This alien has big ears.
This alien has no nose.
This alien I would like to see.
This alien can fly.
This alien is sad.
This alien I would like to see.
This alien can see us.
This alien flies around the sky.

Rebecca Healy (8)
Panshanger School

THIS SHUTTLE

This shuttle has blasted from earth
This shuttle has gone wrong and hit the moon
This shuttle gets all dizzy
This shuttle has had enough of space
This shuttle is back on earth.

James Pethybridge (9)
Panshanger School

PLANETS

Pluto is golden like Mickey Mouse's dog from Disneyland,
Saturn is huge
Bigger than 500 times your hand.
Uranus is full of gold
And silver secrets that can't be told.
Venus is pretty, lovely and sparkly
Beautiful and old.
Mars is full of Mars bars, lovely and smooth.
I wish I could eat one!
It will make one of my teeth gleam.
Jupiter is pink, the colour of your cheeks,
Also the colour of your ears
(I bet it can hear).

Laura Clark (9)
Panshanger School

THIS SUN

This sun has burning hot flames coming out of the side,
It has shone on our country.
Our world has gone round the sun many times
This sun has given light to another country.
Now it has run out of light.

Jenifer Robinson (8)
Panshanger School

THE TIRING JOURNEY TO FRANCE

I was on my way to France
on a ferry.
We stayed the night there.
I couldn't get
to sleep.
When we got there
everybody was speaking French
and I didn't understand
one bit.
On the way back
at night
our van broke down
and the man wouldn't
take our credit card
so we called the house
that we stayed at
and he
and another friend
went to get a gallon
of gas
and we had to wait
one hour
but then
we went back to St Albans.

Alicia Kuczmierczyk (8)
St Adrian's RC JMI School, St Albans

CLICKING

I was at my house
I'm always clicking my fingers
My mum said 'You will get rheumatism'
I
Said
'Nonsense.'
I saw a book, it showed
Rheumatism.
It looked horrible
'And you won't have a boyfriend.'
I thought for a moment.
I said 'I will stop
Clicking
My
Fingers.'
After that I never did click my fingers.

Lydia Mallinson (9)
St Adrian's RC JMI School, St Albans

THE LION

I'm a lion big and strong
My teeth and claws are very long.

When night falls I am about
If you see me, scream and shout.

When daylight comes I'm wide awake,
Come and see me, pay at the gate because Whipsnade is my estate.

Sean Dodge (9)
St Adrian's RC JMI School, St Albans

WHEN I GOT LOST

We went to Toys R Us
We were looking around and I went into a toy house.
I was playing when I heard
'Sian.'
I ran out of there
I felt worried.
I didn't know what to do.
Soon I found my mum.
I was so happy
I would always stay with them.

Sian Connolly (8)
St Adrian's RC JMI School, St Albans

I HURT MY ARM

I hurt my arm at swimming
I hurt it
on the wall.
It hurt very much.
It was
very painful too.
I went
home.
On Monday I
went to
the hospital
to get it bandaged up.

Sophie Anderson (9)
St Adrian's RC JMI School, St Albans

MY FRIEND CHARLOTTE

One day
I got lost in the country.
I tried to find my mum and dad.
But I couldn't find them anywhere.
But then I found my old friend, Charlotte.
I couldn't believe it.
She was lost too.
She was crying
and I was trying to cheer her up.
'I haven't seen you for ages.'
We played I Spy,
talked about school,
told secrets
and talked a bit more.
But then we saw our mums and dads
standing next to a tree right next to us,
talking.

Joanna Lewin (8)
St Adrian's RC JMI School, St Albans

I'M BORED

One, two, three, four, five,
Gardening, cooking, how to stay alive?
Nothing on the telly, don't know what to do,
Shall I do my homework or paint the bathroom blue?
Shall I just sit here and think about tomorrow?
Look on the bright side and away goes my sorrow.

Claire-Louise Hill (9)
St Adrian's RC JMI School, St Albans

MY JOURNEY TO THE ISLE OF WIGHT

It was boring
At first because
We were just driving
For a
Very very very very very very
Long time, driving
To get to the harbour.
At last we were here.
We were going to stay at the Isle of Wight
For two weeks.
We did enjoy it
We were outside on top of the ferry
For two hours.
Then we made our way home.

Michelle Nash (9)
St Adrian's RC JMI School, St Albans

HURT HEAD

One day I was in my bedroom reading when my brother came in.
He said 'Let's go on top of the wardrobe, David.'
'OK' I said
He jumped off
but I didn't.
Eventually I jumped
and cut my forehead.

David Gibbons (8)
St Adrian's RC JMI School, St Albans

HURT

About five years ago
I was with my dad and sister.
I was the only one riding a bike.
Then I started to go
faster
And
faster.
I was shouting 'Come and chase me.'
Then I fell off
my bike.
Firstly my teeth
started to bleed.
My dad and my sister
quickly ran over.
They picked me up
and put me on
my bike.
They pushed me up the hill
to my house.
My dad quickly
rang the orthodontist.

Michael Devine (8)
St Adrian's RC JMI School, St Albans

THE ROTTEN FIVE PENCE

Last Friday I was in my mum's car
and I had five pence.
It tasted lovely,
I thought I might leave it in my mouth
for a while longer.
Then my mum called
'Yes Mum,' I said.
'Please can you help me?'
'Yes' I said.
I ran then I stopped.
I screamed.
'Aaahhh!'
I had swallowed the money.
'Mummmm . . .!
Help.' I felt cold
and empty.
The doctor came down and said I was fine.
It was supposed to be my charity money.
Now I *never* want to see a 5p again.

Sarah Torrens (8)
St Adrian's RC JMI School, St Albans

SPAIN

I went to Spain
on a plane.
We saw a zoo
we went there too.
We had some sweets
for the journey.
We stayed in a villa
near a river.
Lots of bees
in the trees
But after all it was very nice because
we stayed near a river
in a villa
in Spain.

Nicola Rudd (9)
St Adrian's RC JMI School, St Albans

HOW I LOST MY TEETH

When I was four,
I used to play
Silly games on the stairs.
One day I was hiding from my sister.

I fell down the stairs
I hit each step
As I went down.

Thump!

I'd hit the wall
I was rushed to hospital,
Within a week my mum
Found out and said to me,
'Your teeth went back up your gum'
I couldn't eat for ages.

And that's how I lost my teeth.

Jonathan Liddle (9)
St Adrian's RC JMI School, St Albans

NEW YEAR'S EVE

On New Year's Eve
I went to a restaurant
When I got there
I was bursting for the toilet
so I quickly went to the toilet.
When I got in there it was so stinky I had to hold my nose
whenever I went in there.
When it came to dinnertime I was really hungry
but the vegetarians had to eat first
so I had to wait till after midnight
when I went to get my food.
By accident I knocked over a plate with loads of food on.
Then I quickly ran to the toilet
where it stunk badly.
When I came out everyone was laughing
and I went down to sit with my cousins.

Krina Patel (9)
St Adrian's RC JMI School, St Albans

LOST

I went to Weymouth in the summer,
And we stayed in a caravan.
My favourite was the go-karts,
But early one morning we went fishing,
Then we went to Weymouth market,
But when I was tying my laces,
My mum went away,
And I went *all* my way round the market,
I thought she had run away,
And when I got back to the toy stall I said,
'I
  cannot
     find
        my
           mum
             and
               dad.'
No time to answer
My mum came running round really fast crying.
My dad told me off,
But
I explained.

Robert Tominey (8)
St Adrian's RC JMI School, St Albans

COUGH SWEETS

I hate those horrid cough sweets
your mum gives you when you're ill.
I hate those icky things,
they're worse than any pill.
You put them in your mouth
and as soon as they've begun
that very nasty hot taste
explodes upon your tongue!
You push them up and down,
from side to side to make them go.
But no matter how hard you try,
they just seem to grow and grow.
And when they're nearly over
and you're feeling rather glad,
your mum gives you another one,
which makes you rather sad!
I hate those horrid cough sweets!
(and the only way to win
is when your mum's not looking,
throw them in the
bin!)

Naomi Brice (8)
St Adrian's RC JMI School, St Albans

SNOWMAN

Snowman big, snowman fat,
looming over the garden cat.
Snowdrops falling everywhere,
nothing can beat that snowman's stare.
He has a hat and scarf,
pieces of coal for eyes and mouth.
He has a carrot for his nose . . .
something keeps nibbling it,
who? No one knows!
He has little ears made of garden pegs,
twigs for arms and snow for legs.
I go to bed and wonder why,
Why, oh why, can't my
Snowman come alive!

Sam Brzeski (9)
St Adrian's RC JMI School, St Albans

COSMIC MAN

Have you heard of cosmic man?
I'm sure you have - you'll know this man.
He nips about the school at night
to check that everything's alright.
He always does his very best,
but I think he should take a rest.
He paints the walls
and cleans the floors.
He's always there to open doors.
I'm sure you've guessed, I've given clues!
Now you know when your pipes are dripping,
why don't you call for Mr Tipping!
(Mr Tipping is the school caretaker).

Charlotte Shannon-Little (9)
St Adrian's RC JMI School, St Albans

DADDIES

Some daddies are fat
and some are thin.
Some daddies are tall
and some are small.
Some are nice
and some are not at all!
Some are hairy -
and some are lairy!
Some are bad
and some are mad.
If you look north, south
east or west,
You would find my dad
is the very best!

Sophie Lovett (8)
St Adrian's RC JMI School, St Albans

ALL THE KIDS GO OUT TO PLAY

All the kids go out to play
Every single Tuesday,
On Monday Julie's playing the trumpet,
On Wednesday Tim goes to football,
On Thursday Jess and Ben go swimming,
On Friday Holly plays netball at school,
Saturday Karen has a club meeting,
And Sunday they're all at church,
So there's only gorgeous, glamorous Tuesday left.

Eleanor Sheridan (9)
St Dominic RC JMI School, Harpenden

THE BOYS' BEDROOM

Twelve caps on the bedpost,
Lego on the floor,
Trains set out on train tracks,
Posters on the door.
Photos of first birthdays
In the morning,
Looked at in dismay,
Well overflowing bins,
On the carpet,
Many empty biscuit tins.
In toy boxes there are toy cars,
There is a toy spaceship,
Toy aliens from Mars,
Minute micro figures,
Taxis, buses and even diggers.
An untidy bed,
Perched upon it, his little bear, Ted.
Sweet wrappers around the room,
Picking them up is a mother's doom.

Ciàràn Owens (9)
St Dominic RC JMI School, Harpenden

DAD

He didn't like the racket so he
caught me by the jacket,
I said, 'Dad, one of us has got to go.
It's my dance music or your noise
which makes me sick
so I don't see why I have to go.'
He pushed me and he pulled me
and he stretched me like a tree.
I said 'Dad if you like
I'll go and play on my bike'
And that's when I felt really low.

He caught me in a flash
with a rolled-up paper bash
which landed on my head just so.
So now you know,
it was me who had to go.

Christen Williams (9)
St Dominic RC JMI School, Harpenden

UP IN SPACE

Up in space,
it's a very slow race.
Things floating around,
without a sound.
All lonely and cold,
nowhere to walk
I've been told.
That's what it is like up in space.

Up in space,
it's a wonderful place.
Up in the stars
there's a planet called Mars.
Pluto the smallest,
Jupiter the tallest.
That's what it's like up in space.

Up in space
you have a very slow pace.
The moon glows,
everything flows.
Rockets blast,
ever so fast.
That's what it's like up in space.

Helen Bentley (10)
St Dominic RC JMI School, Harpenden

ALL ABOUT

Chemistry's all about atoms,
Physics is all about cars,
History's all about conquerors,
And astronomy's all about stars.

Cookery's all about cooking,
Geography's all about towns,
Science is all about forces,
Maths is all about rounds.

Art is all about paintings,
Mixing colours as well,
So many subjects I'm learning,
I feel like I'm stuck down a well!

Andrew Kelly (9)
St Dominic RC JMI School, Harpenden

THE WIND

Howling, growling, rushing wind,
Like a hurricane it is,
A little breeze not for long,
Twirling, whistling, rushing wind,
It is like a wolf howling on a cliff.

Howling, growling, rushing wind,
A little wind, not for long,
It's like a dragon,
Howling, growling, rushing wind.

Emma Creighton (9)
St Dominic RC JMI School, Harpenden

THE CHOCOLATE FACTORY

Melted chocolate, marshmallow and fudge
Swirling r
     o
      u
       n
       d
       a
      n
      d
      r
      o
       u
        n
           d and round in a giant steel volcano.

Runny caramel oozing and dripping from a
large round tap   *drip*
        drop
          drip!

Walnuts moving on a conveyor belt
being dropped into a bubbling swimming pool
of delicious creamy chocolate   *plop*
            plop
         plop, plop!

Melted chocolate rolled out
to make thin, crispy sandwich layers
with a lovely vanilla cream spurting out the sides.

All through the chocolate factory,
delicious smells of toffee, chocolate and fudge
wafting through the floorboards.

How I love the chocolate factory!

Louise Thompson (9)
St Dominic RC JMI School, Harpenden

OH RATS

I'd like to be a small grey rat
Eating cheese and crumbs
Nibble, nibble, maybe one dribble
And not have to do all those sums. Yes!

I'd like to be a small grey rat
Down in the sewers I'd go
Exploring for hours with my new powers
To quickly scuttle away - tiptoe.

The day came when I had had my tea
A witch's spell was put on me
Which made me turn into a rat
A small grey one, I say, in fact.

I ate cheese and crumbs
I didn't do my sums (that was the best bit)
I explored for hours
I did it with my powers.

But then I came out of the drain
I saw a foot, I lay in pain!
The foot went up and after that
It came back down and I went *splat!*

I'm now in rat heaven
I've been here for the years of seven
And now my strongest memory
Is . . . *I hate the foot that stepped on me!*

Adam Davies (9)
St Dominic RC JMI School, Harpenden

THE SEA

Precious pearls
Washing waves
As the sharks
Rule the sea
The sea turtles swim slowly
Lay their eggs
Off to an unknown country
Angel fish, a school of them.

The wildlife is polluted
Acid rain soil spills.
It spells disaster for the fish
Some people wonder how they survive.

Matthew Whitworth (9)
St Dominic RC JMI School, Harpenden

ZAPPING THROUGH SPACE

Zapping through the stars
In a bright red open spaceship
Over Mars we go
Bumping all the way
Icicles on Saturn's ring
Making all the stars shine
What fun it is to stop and chant
a *zapping* poem tonight!

Rebecca Costello (9)
St John's CE JMI School, Welwyn Garden City

METEORITE

M assive pieces of rock float around in space.
E xtra bits sometimes fall and come crashing to Earth.
T errible things happen when they hit houses.
E normous meteorites the size of London are very bad.
O rbiting over planets is rarely seen around Earth.
R ather rarely do you see them in England, quite a lot in America.
I think meteorites are fabulous to see, but not nice to be hit by.
T ough pieces of rock can smash through a car roof.
E xciting meteorites are still very dangerous.

Benjamin John Cole (9)
St John's CE JMI School, Welwyn Garden City

MARS

M artians go mad.
A liens go mad, bonkers and crazy.
R ockets blast-off into space.
S pace is spooky.

Chris Humphreys (9)
St John's CE JMI School, Welwyn Garden City

GOING TO THE MOON YOU KNOW

3, 2, 1 blast-off the rocket
has taken off. It's going to
the moon, you know.
They will see all the stars
as they go past them.

Then they got there.
They said 'Hooray, we are here,'
and they put a flag in the moon.
It went right through the moon,
the moon said 'Ouch, that hurt the people!'

They turned and fell off
the moon, you know, and
they landed in a river,
and they went all the way
to the sea.

And they were never seen again
you know.

Geoffrey Pritchard (8)
St John's CE JMI School, Welwyn Garden City

WILL I EVER KNOW?

Who is God married to?
Will he ever die?
Is there such a thing as dog heaven?
When will the Earth blow up?
Will I ever learn my tables?
How many stars in the universe?
Will the Earth ever crash into the sun?
Does he really like me?

Grant Hailey (9)
St Margaret Clitherow RC School, Stevenage

I LOVE YOU

I love you, music,
even though you hurt my ears.
I love you, pig,
even though you stink.
I love you, Mum,
even though you shout at me.
I love you, sun,
even though you hurt my eyes.
I love you, caterpillar,
even though you tickle me.
I love you, rubber,
even though you make my work messy.

Elizabeth Mulhall (7)
St Margaret Clitherow RC School, Stevenage

TEACHER

He's a very royal gold,
the electrifying loud buzz,
the very nicest Cadbury's chocolate bar
waiting to be discovered.
He's a lively kangaroo hopping, bouncing and having fun.
He's Alan Shearer on Match of the Day,
a happy storm passing, creating clouds,
a wobbly-looking chair.
He's a comfortable pair of climbing boots
hoping to be worn.

Andrew Kennedy (9)
St Margaret Clitherow RC School, Stevenage

I LOVE YOU

I love you, teacher,
even though you give me hard work.
I love you, Ross,
even though you break my model.
I love you, Mummy,
even though you have smelly feet.
I love you, fish,
even though you don't walk.
I love you, Daddy,
even though you've got hairs on your face.
I love you, pencil,
even though you make me do messy writing.
I love you, legs,
even though you don't make me run fast.

Ryan Inglis (7)
St Margaret Clitherow RC School, Stevenage

THE UNANSWERABLE

Will I ever get another chance to live?
When will every single person die?
Who will be the last person to live?
What would life be like if everything was dead?
Would I be myself if I wasn't alive?
Would I ever be someone after I'd died?

Sam Harte (8)
St Margaret Clitherow RC School, Stevenage

I LOVE YOU

I love you, Lotty,
Even though you jump a lot.
I love you, blackcurrant,
even though you don't fizz.
I love you shoes,
even though you get dirty.
I love you, Dad,
even though you don't play games with me.
I love you, Mum,
even though you send me up to my bedroom.
I love you birds,
even though you tweet a lot.
I love you, work,
even though you make me bored.
I love you, friends,
even though we break up.
I love you, Robert,
even though you annoy me.
I love you, Graham,
even though you don't take me to the shops.

Bethany McGloin (7)
St Margaret Clitherow RC School, Stevenage

FROST IS COMING

Frost is coming
Winter's on the way
Everyone is happy
Wanting to play

The sun sets in the sky
And the snow melts alive
It makes the night
Look like day.

When our parents say goodnight
I think of lovely things
Of making snowmen
And making heart warming things.

Morning comes,
I take my warm dreams
And go so happy
Playing in the snow.

Sarah Hill (9)
Sacred Heart School

LOOKING INTO AN ICE WORLD

You can see a forest in a ball
There's a house with iceberg steps,
A jungle of ice tigers with an
Ice moon to tell us it's night.
The stars sparkle, it's never day
It keeps on glittering away.
A child is feeding a bird with
A silver beak, snow is falling to the ground.
People, more and more people come out to fetch
The snowflakes from the ground.
They take it home and fry it.
It never melts. It's going wrinkly.
A volcano has erupted and land is coming
And changes to colours instead of white.
New life begins!

Jenny Campbell (8)
Sacred Heart School

QUIETER THAN...

Quieter than a mouse,
Quieter than a house.
Quieter than a feather,
Quieter than my friend, Heather.

Quieter than a box,
Quieter than a fox.
Quieter than the rain,
Quieter than the drain.

Quieter than a stool,
Quieter than a pool.
Quieter than a newspaper being read,
Quieter than my sister going to bed.

That's how quiet my mum and dad want me to be.

Not a chance!

Helen Lawrence (9)
Sacred Heart School

SUMMER

Summer is a time for fun and play
Summer is a time for a very happy day
Summer is a time for loving and caring
Summer is a time for kindness and sharing
Summer is a time for happiness and joy
Summer is a time for every girl and boy
Summer is a time for
        Friendship!

Louise Frost (8)
Sacred Heart School

ANIMALS

A polar bear does not live in heat
A horse can do a magnificent leap
A sheepdog can round up lots of sheep.

Animals
Animals
Animals

A cat pounces on its prey
A cow munches grass all day
And parrots repeat what you say.

Animals
Animals
Animals

Herbivores are very lazy
Bees like flowers including daisies
Big hyenas laugh like crazy.

Animals
Animals
Animals

Olivia Jane Ferrigan (8)
Sacred Heart School

In The Day Of The Life Of A Schoolgirl

The weekend's gone and the day has just begun
In the day of the life of a schoolgirl
It's Monday, the start of a new adventurous week
With hopes, fears and worries.
What a bore biology and more, maths, English and art.
In the day of the life of a schoolgirl.
Ding dong goes the bell, lunchtime everyone.
All in one the children run, to get to the dinner hall first.
'Yes please,' 'No, thank you,' 'That one would be nice.'
In the day of the life of a schoolgirl.
Lunch goes, games come, netball everyone.
'Pass, Anne,' 'Shoot, Jane,'
Final score 2-1.
In the day of the life of a schoolgirl.
Ding dong goes the bell, home time, everyone.
'Bye, Miss,' shout the girls running out of school.

Jianna Miserotti (9)
Sacred Heart School

My Rainbow Kite

My kite is made of rainbow
It sweeps across the sky
I can almost touch it
If I really try.
A flock of birds
Smash through it
And tear across its threads
Now my beautiful rainbow
Is slap upon my head.

Thomas Gibbons (9)
Sacred Heart School

GOOD MORNING SCHOOL.

I say 'Good morning' to my teacher,
Before I start my day,
Hang my coat upon its peg,
And off I go on my way

I walk up the marble stairs,
To the top floor,
And greet my friends,
As I go through the classroom door.

I sharpen my pencil,
Get out my books,
Do my work,
As the teacher talks and looks.

Out on the playground.
Having fun,
Chatting and playing,
With everyone.

Having my lunch,
Yum, yum, yum.
Nicely packed,
By my mum.

It's home time now,
Looking forward to dinner,
I love my school,
It's a winner.

Sara Noone (9)
Sacred Heart School

CHOCOLATE

Chocolate, chocolate
yummy yum yum
It has to go straight
in my tum.

Big bars, small bars
soft and creamy
brown or white
oh so dreamy.

Chocolate, chocolate
yummy yum yum
melting on my fingers
licking my thumb.

Caramel, nuts, raisins and more
anywhere
anytime
you I adore.

Chocolate, chocolate
yummy yum yum
ruining my teeth
sticking on my gum.

Hard centres, soft centres
just open the lid
give me another
I'm the Milky Bar Kid.

Stuart Jordan (8)
Sacred Heart School

TRAVELLING SNAKE

Hello, I'm Sammy
I'm golden, wriggly and small
I've been round the world
Without a ticket at all.
I slid into a suitcase
And ended up in Dublin
Then someone tried me on
They thought I was a bracelet
I got taken to America.
I then got stuck on someone's shoe
And off again I flew
Ending up in Paris
I got fed up with that
So I slid around
Someone's hat and ended up
In a tulip in Amsterdam.
I got taken in a bunch
To London,
Phew I'm home again.
Bye, from Sammy.

Hazel Boland-Shanahan (9)
Sacred Heart School

SEAS

It's warm and hot
There are no drops.
People are bathing
At the Mediterranean Sea.

Children making sandcastles and
Babies toddle to knock them down.
The cries of seagulls circling
And the feel of the cool breeze.
At the English Channel.

People bobbing all around
They cannot sink at all
Mud is plastered on their bodies.
It looks like a strange holiday
At the Black Sea.

Hot sun, no clouds
Palm trees fringe the beach,
Lines and lines of sun chairs
And people lying on them
At the Indian Ocean.

Marisa Rabbini (9)
Sacred Heart School

Red Dragon

As the red dragon lies by the big waterfall
It lies still, staring
Its tongue on the rough stone
Lying motionless.
All he hears is the waterfall.
Hunters in the background
Going over the rocks
Looking for the dragon.
Going, going, looking for that dragon.
One by one,
More and more
The hunters come.
Shouting, waving swords in the air.
Soon a battle may begin
Just the dragon and the hunters.

Niall Galvin (9)
Two Waters School

Snow

Swirling, twirling
Down from the sky.
Splat! On the ground they go.
The snowflakes flutter down
So white, so cold.
Swerving through the sky.
So soft, so crunchy.

Oliver Martin (8)
Two Waters School

SNOW

Snow whirls in the sky
And glides along the floor.
Snowballs go splat!
Blizzards whirl in the sky
And snow drifts to the ground.
Snow crunches under your feet.
A snowman stands still.
Snow makes your hand numb.
When it is bitterly cold, your nose goes red.
When it gets dark the snowflakes twinkle.
Then it is brilliant.

Joshua Taylor (8)
Two Waters School

SNOW

Cold snowflakes floating and twirling
In the frozen sky.
Twinkling and shining in the night sky.
It twinkles, it glides in the night sky
And down it slides.
Whee! Whoo! Twinkle like a star
Floating down to the ground
Till it goes flat.
The cold night is very flat
Until those snowflakes glide down.

Nicholas Mills (8)
Two Waters School

THE DRAGON

The dragon wanders peacefully,
Through the never ending green.
He sees a mouse and he eats it,
The blood tastes better than it seems.

A thousand bugs,
All captured by the dragon's giant talons.
His fiery breathing sounds loudly
He can hardly keep his balance.

He is tired,
Lays his head down,
On some smoking fiery rocks.
It has a lot of static and lets off some
Tiny shocks.

Scales upon his back
And fire upon his breath.
The very tired dragon,
He lays down to rest.

Sam Nicholls (9)
Two Waters School

SNOW

The snow is cold and slippery.
Snowflakes whisper down from the sky.
Snow twinkles in the night.
Snow swirls around the garden
And you slip around.

Jason Remmington (8)
Two Waters School

THE NIGHTMARE

I close my eyes,
I begin to dream.
I'm going through a black hole.
It's whizzing in circles.
It's dizzy and black.
Chairs and tables flying.
Hang on! A sudden thud!
I hit the ground.
Things come towards me.
Hair, hair everywhere!
Then I'm trapped.
No light!
I'm trapped.
No life!

Lara Peasnell (9)
Two Waters School

SNOW

Snowflakes go round fast in the sky.
Snow falls slowly from the sky.
The snow falls fast on the snowman.
Snowballs zoom along the ground.
Gloves protect you from the snow.
It is cold and crunchy.

Billy Dove (8)
Two Waters School

MARIGOLD

As the golden yellow sun sets down,
And as the time turns later,
I climb across the rocks.
The rocks are hot,
Boiling my feet.
I slip.
Then I look below me.
I am scared,
The water is rushing along down the stream.
My foot fell in -
I grab the rock again.
I can feel the water pulling me down.
I hear my mother call
'Oh Marigold, oh Marigold, time for tea!'
'Mum' I call back, there is no reply.
If these rocks get any hotter,
I shall fall.
So I close my eyes.
I jump.
It's all murky.
My leg looks red, the water is turning red.
Then all of a sudden,
It goes completely dark.
As I drift down the stream -
So frightened!

Jody Coffey (9)
Two Waters School

FEAR

As the old wooden stairs
Fell before me.
I crashed down to the floor.
I lay still on the cold and wet floor.
'Get up' a voice said
but I couldn't.
It felt like 1000 bricks
had fallen on top of me.
'Mum!' I called, but there was no reply
I called again 'Mum!'
But it was no good.
I could hear my voice fading
Where the cobwebs had covered my mouth.

Lauren Morris (9)
Two Waters School

ANGELS

Angels coming to God
Who is
Delivering news to all parts of the world.
Retaining a big halo over their heads.
Sitting motionless in the sky.
But when it's time to lay their heads and go into the real world.
They wake up from their fearless dream and
Smell the sweet fresh air.

Charlotte Wright (9)
Two Waters School

San Francisco Bay

The house off the cliff,
The Pacific Ocean
Just looking under the bay.
The Golden Gate Bridge
Across the ocean
With the cars going past.
The scintillating moon
Glooming over the bay
And the mountains shining with mist,
Setting the whole scene.

When night has passed
The blazing ships sail in.
The house that looks like a shell,
The flashy cars zooming
Out of the house.
Then it's night.
The whole place is silent.
All you can hear are the waves
Tossing around.
The amazing lights of the bay
Dying out until it's day.

Jonathan Munday (9)
Two Waters School